Violence in Children:
spark, tinder, fuel

Alan M. Davick, M.D.

Violence in Children: *spark, tinder, fuel*
Alan M. Davick, M.D.
© 2016 Alan M. Davick, M.D.
ISBN: 978-0-9890053-9-5

MISKIDDING, LLC
P.O. Box 101127
Cape Coral, FL 33910-1127
URL: www.DrDavick.com
Blog: www.MisbehaviorInKids.com
Email: miskidding1@gmail.com

Acknowledgments

Many of the principles presented in this book are distilled from the **MIS/Kidding Process**®, published separately in **Managing Misbehavior in Kids**: *The MIS/kidding Process*® - *A Professionals' Manual*, from **Bullying**: *Rarely Travels Alone* and **Discipline Your Child**: *Without going to jail*, each developed and written by the author after many years of collaboration with colleagues in the fields of Medicine, Psychology and Education and from consultations with many families in distress.

The author wishes to express his ongoing gratitude to Rik Feeney, author, editor, publisher and coach, whose unfailing professionalism and irreplaceable friendship elevated the writing of this book to the level of a feast on bourbon chicken.

To Barbara, my wife and life support and to Tilly, my constant canine companion, a hearty thanks.

Al Davick
Cape Coral, FL

Table of Contents

Preface

One of the most common reasons parents bring their child to my office is someone's complaint of violent behavior by their child. Parents, guardians or others have become concerned, frightened, even threatened by the behavior. Sometimes, the behavior has gone so far as to involve police or courts.

Strangely, some forms of violence may not be recognized as such. Bullying, lying, oppositional behaviors, cruelty to animals, stealing, cutting oneself and other forms of self-harm are examples of violent behaviors often assigned lower levels of significance than fighting, punching, stabbing, property destruction and fire-setting. But all are forms of violence, any one of which may lead to someone's injury or death. And all these behaviors are manifestations of anger.

In this book, we'll liken the occurrence of violent behavior to the setting of a fire. We'll learn to recognize events that trigger anger, circumstances that ignite rage and underlying child vulnerabilities that fuel violence -

sparks, tinder and fuel. And of course, we'll see how to extinguish violent behavior.

If you're a parent, you'll likely need to get professional assistance – at the right time and of the right kind- to manage underlying mental health vulnerabilities. This book will guide you through that process.

With this book you won't need to be a professional child specialist to recognize your child's violent behavior or to organize its management.

Introduction

Violent behavior in children is triggered by the elevation of anger into rage. Anger may be justified, as in cases of the bullying of a child by a peer or by the chance occurrence of a life-long medical condition like diabetes, or it may be an inappropriate response to a trivial constraint, like temporarily restricting the use of a computer at bedtime.

Not all anger leads to rage. Indeed, by 5 years of age, most children are beginning to handle anger with strategies they've learned from their guardians – like talking, complaining or negotiating with their guardians. And even when anger morphs into rage and leaves no time for using strategies or is too intense to be contained, violence may be inner-directed, leading to a child's withdrawal, disengagement from normal activities and suicidal acts.

Whether anger is justified or not, its level of intensity determines the likelihood of dangerous consequences. Understanding why a child is angry or enraged doesn't mean danger is lessened. And removing all triggers to anger is impossible. But, if action is taken to douse anger by altering or removing situations that act as tinder and managing underlying mental health issues that fuel anger's conversion to rage, violent behavior can be avoided.

Since anger can progress to rage, then to violence, removing or treating the causes of a child's anger will eliminate violent behavior. It's often possible to change circumstances that ignite anger. An environment of neglect or abuse, financial issues or personality conflicts with teachers act as tinder igniting anger and initiating a sequence of events leading to violence.

Underlying vulnerabilities, often accessible only by child specialists, like brain damage, genetic inheritance or mental disorders, can add fuel to anger, progress to violence and resist elimination.

Here are some examples of common circumstances and mental health disorders capable of igniting anger and fueling rage in children:

Potentially reversible circumstances acting as tinder and igniting anger:

- Victimization – like being bullied

- Inappropriate models – like violent behavior of parents or siblings

- Drug use – removes inhibitions

- Educational failure – learning problems

- Family financial issues – restricted play, recreational activities

- Ill-equipped guardians – like aged foster parents physically unable to act as parents

Here are some irreversible causes of anger acting to fuel rage and requiring counseling, therapy, medications or acceptance:

- Inherited mental disorders

- Brain damage

- Irreversible events – like death of parents or friends

In the chapters that follow, we'll learn to recognize triggers to anger – the sparks that begin the ignition sequence leading to violence. We'll see almost any normal event in a child's life can spark ignition. So removing all triggers to anger is virtually impossible.

Though we can't shield a vulnerable child from all the normal events capable of sparking anger, we can control much of the child's environment – the tinder upon which triggers act to ignite anger.

Most importantly, we can identify, manage and sometimes remove a child's vulnerability to rage, like brain damage or mental health disorders - fuels that morph anger into rage, then violent behavior.

Chapter One

All about anger

Recognizing Anger

In my experience, most children express anger in ways parents and other observers can easily recognize. Body language, including facial expressions, tensing of extremities and changes in the quality of voice, usually broadcast children's emotional state.

When anger isn't obvious

A number of mental disorders disconnect the presence of anger from typical expressions of body language. In such instances, anger may flourish with little or no indication of its presence. Examples include self-injurious behaviors like cutting and hair pulling or obsessive-compulsive rituals like the unending rearrangement of items in the home blocking scheduled activities.

Parents' responses to anger may or may not be effective

Most parents intuitively attempt to lessen anger in a child, recognizing its consequences could be disruptive or even harmful to the child or others. Parents' responses are usually appropriate, but sometimes inappropriate.

Appropriate responses, which usually reduce anger, include kind words or a show of affection. Inappropriate responses, which often intensify anger, include punishment or mockery.

Can anger be useful?

Think about the last time you were angry. You probably didn't think self-critically – nothing was *your* fault. You might have taken pleasure in seeing the person(s) you targeted step back as if in fear of you. You might even have experienced a feeling of power in the moment.

Children experience these effects of anger as well as adults. Anger may temporarily reduce or eliminate poor self-esteem or feelings of vulnerability. These effects may become addictive for some children, prompting them to use anger to defend against perceived (or real) shortcomings. For example, bullying is often fueled by self-ignited anger.

In spite of short-term benefits children may experience from anger, this emotion burdens many physical processes in the body, including blood pressure, heart rate, metabolic activity and even immune activity. In general, chronic anger is harmful and may ultimately shorten life.

Rage – an intense level of anger

When anger reaches the level of rage, it's out of control. Indeed, the appearance of a child experiencing rage is almost indistinguishable from that of an epileptic child having a seizure (convulsion). Eyes may roll, drooling may occur, extremities may flail, strange sounds may be heard. Carrying on a conversation with a child in a rage is impossible. During a rage a child may even fall the floor, kicking and shrieking, much as an epileptic child might.

Many of the changes seen in the body of a child in rage are caused by the release of adrenaline, a hormone responsible for the "fight or flight" reaction to danger (let's imagine a lion in the living room!). Eyes widen to allow better vision in poor light, heart rate and blood pressure increase to allow greater muscular strength and speed, thinking accelerates such that children may later describe "time slowing down." These powerful effects may become addictive to some children who purposefully trigger rage to experience them.

In some children, mental disorders propel anger to rage with triggers most parents would consider trivial – like requesting a child to clean a messy room or set a table. In these situations, with underlying mental health disorders, anger may morph into rage, then explode into inward or outwardly directed violence.

Two forms of anger – situational (curable) vs. brain-imposed abnormalities (treatable)

Anger can be divided into two main categories. Some forms of anger are caused by situations occurring in a child's environment or by a child's chosen reaction to such situations, some of which include the victimization of bullying or the divorce of parents. These causes can either be eliminated or managed by strategies children can learn to apply (as in the case of bullying), or the unity of divorced parents in setting consistent rules and offering appropriate forms of affection (as in the case of divorce).

Other forms of anger, though also manageable, cannot so easily be contained. They are imposed by abnormal brain processes, either acquired, like some types of brain damage, or inherited, as for example Bipolar Disorder. Here follow some examples from each category.

"Curable" causes of anger

Some of the most common situations I see in my office acting as tinder to the ignition of anger in children and which can be either eliminated or managed with appropriate strategies, are:

- Parents' separation and/or divorce

- Physical or sexual abuse

- Neglect or abandonment by guardian(s)

- Moving to a new neighborhood with separation from friends

- Bullying by parents, siblings or peers

- Change of schools

- Birth of a sibling

- Demands on parents imposed by a disabled sibling

- Death of a loved one – parent, sibling, friend

• Excessive punishment as a means of discipline

Brain-imposed (though treatable) causes of anger – manageable, but not curable

Here are some brain-imposed conditions which create a vulnerability to intense anger and act as fuel to violence in children. Though these conditions cannot (yet) be reversed, the progression of anger to rage in these conditions can be slowed or blocked with medication:

• Brain damage - either from birth or from events occurring after birth, like meningitis

• Mental disorders, like Bipolar Disorder or Intermittent Explosive Disorder

• Psychogenic Non-Epileptic Seizures – seizure-like rages, often with normal EEG (brainwave test)

Triggers (sparks) vs. tinder (accelerants) in the ignition of anger

Accelerants are substances that promote or intensify fire. Examples include sawdust, gasoline and propane. Just as accelerants promote or intensify fire, intense anger or rage promote violence. Accelerants require ignition – like a spark or heat – to begin burning. Once a fire is ignited, fuel is required to sustain it. Similarly, violence requires the accelerant of intense anger to be ignited by a triggering event. Without the accelerant, a spark is unlikely to ignite a fire. Without an environment acting as an accelerant (tinder), or an underlying mental health vulnerability acting as fuel, triggering events are unlikely to ignite anger, progress to rage or lead to violence.

Reduce violent behavior by targeting the development of intense anger

All children experience anger. One measure of children's maturation is their ability to control anger. Children may inherit or acquire vulnerabilities which render the control of anger difficult or impossible. Inherited vulnerabilities include mental disorders like Bipolar Disorder other Mood Disorders and certain forms of Mental Retardation. Acquired vulnerabilities include certain situations or events, like bullying, poverty or the diversion of parenting from one child to a sibling with disabilities.

A vulnerability to anger and its conversion to violent behavior requires a triggering event, often trivial in nature. A list of triggering events would include almost all daily human activities, such as asking a child to clean up for dinner, put clothes in a hamper or get ready for school. Attempts to eliminate these potential triggers of anger in children who are vulnerable to rage and violence are doomed to failure. Rather than attempting to eliminate any activities or requests potentially triggering anger, we must focus on reducing situations or events and underlying vulnerabilities that ignite or fuel intense anger.

Examples of mistakes parents (and politicians) make in managing violence

Let me give you some examples of misguided attempts to manage anger in children. In each scenario, triggering events (normal life activities) are mistakenly targeted for elimination rather than situations (tinder) igniting anger or underlying vulnerabilities fueling rage and leading to violence. Avoiding one triggering event merely allows another to take its place whereas managing or eliminating inflammable situations or vulnerabilities renders triggers harmless.

Johnny is hitting his infant sister

Violence: Johnny has begun to hit his baby sister in her crib. Whenever his parents catch Johnny trying to hit her, they place him in a covered playpen in his room for half an hour. They hope this punishment will stop the violent behavior.

Fuel: Johnny is 3 years old. He is dependent on parents for nurturance.

Tinder: Last month his Mom gave birth to baby sister, Jill, and now divides her time between the 2 children.

Spark: Mom breast feeds Jill several times a day.

Discussion: Johnny's anger is fueling violent behavior. Breast feeding baby Jill is the triggering event. Fueling Johnny's anger and inflaming it to rage is Johnny's (very appropriate for his age) dependency on his parents for love and affection. Eliminating the sight of Mom breast feeding Jill (by removing Johnny from the room) is an attempt to remove this trigger to violence, but alternative triggers, like Mom washing the baby or holding the baby will just as easily ignite the same response from Johnny.

The solution: Manage or eliminate the tinder igniting Johnny's anger. You may realize Johnny's anger comes from shifting much of Mom's attention from Johnny to his sister. And when Johnny is punished for his behavior, his anger is intensified.

We can't eliminate the trigger (breast feeding). We can't eliminate the fuel (Johnny's age and his need for nurturance). But we can manage the tinder, without which trigger and fuel are harmless. Here's how-

Breast feeding Jill can be transformed into an opportunity for Johnny to receive extra affection (nurturance) from either Mom or Dad. Mom could serve Johnny some ice cream while she feeds Jill. She might allow Johnny to be the "big brother helper", assisting her in holding Jill during feeds. Dad might take Johnny to the park to play "like big boys do." Converting breast feeding time into a period of extra nurturance for Johnny and avoiding punishments that intensify anger are effective strategies to lessen anger.

<u>Alexandra has a short temper and is cutting herself</u>

Alexandra is 15 years of age and just lost a close friend to suicide. She has always been an above average student, but since the death of her friend, grades have fallen to a failing level. Of greatest concern to her parents is their discovery of multiple superficial cuts on her forearms, which she admits she inflicts on herself with a paper clip "when I get angry."

Alexandra doesn't appear depressed and she denies thinking of ending her life. But her parents note she is

now extremely short-tempered and she exhibits angry responses to almost any request, especially performing homework for school.

Alexandra's parents remove her bedroom door to make it harder for her to cut herself without their knowledge. They arrange to home school her to ensure more constant observation. The result is more cutting and more intense anger flare-ups.

Violence: Cutting herself

Fuel: Suicide death of a friend and (as yet) unrecognized depression

Tinder: Anger provoked by Alexandra's feelings of loss and the unfairness of her friend's death

Spark: Demands of school and homework

Discussion: Here's another example of misguided attempts to eliminate triggers to anger. Though the demands of school, including homework, seem to lead to Alexandra's cutting of her forearms, these demands are mere triggers to anger, created by the suicide death of her friend.

It isn't necessary for parents (or the reader) to analyze psychological or psychiatric causes for violent behavior. Such assessments fall within the province of child specialists. But it is important for parents to seek professional assistance when the causes of anger are beyond simple solutions.

Effective strategies for reducing and eventually eliminating the tinder and fuel of Alexandra's anger include psychotherapy and possibly medication. Invading her privacy and withdrawing her from public school are ineffective strategies which merely target triggering events.

When is anger a problem?

No one would doubt anger is a problem when it leads to violence. But can anger present enough of a problem to warrant treatment when it's not leading to violence?

Anger affects many internal processes in the body. Over time, these effects can lead to poor health, even life endangering disturbances. The most effective way to decide if anger needs to be treated is to measure its consequences on the child's behavior.

Anger becomes significant when it leads to misbehavior. As we noted above, many forms of misbehavior don't advertise the presence of anger as a root cause. In many cases, mental health disorders fueled by anger will require child specialists for diagnosis. So, for parents, recognizing misbehavior in any of its guises is the first step in managing expressions of anger.

In Chapter Two let's learn an easy way to recognize and characterize the severity of misbehavior from any cause in children.

Chapter Two

Recognizing & judging the severity of misbehavior

Recognizing misbehavior due to anger (or any other cause) – measuring its consequences

Misbehavior worthy of intervention, including that due to anger, can be identified by examining three Areas of Consequence: effects on Performance, Others, Authority:

Three observable ill consequences of misbehavior fueled by anger

•Inability to perform: When anger is either a lasting emotion (chronic) or when it frequently escalates into rage (high intensity), it will interfere with children's performance in any or all of the following skill areas:

oPhysical health – like stamina and strength

oAbility to learn, or to consistently demonstrate their intelligence – like achieving developmental milestones (e.g.: potty training. Passing grades)

oSocial skills – able to enjoy relationships with others

Misbehavior, including that due to anger, expressing itself through depressed performance requires intervention.

•Complaints from others: Misbehavior due to chronic or intense anger and interfering with peaceful relationships, generating complaints from others, requires intervention. The more diverse the groups who complain about children's misbehavior, the greater the need for intervention. For example, complaints about a child's misbehavior solely from a brother or sister is less likely to require management than complaints from teachers, neighbors or police. Misbehavior in the form of rage may threaten the safety of a child or the safety of others.

•Threats to Authority: Misbehavior fueled by anger typically results in the breaking of rules. Examples range from disrespect of parents or teachers to, lying, stealing, fire-setting or worse.

In general, the greater the number of Areas of Consequence affected by misbehavior, whether fueled by anger or not, the more pressing the need to intervene. When misbehavior affects all three Areas of Consequence, it should be considered potentially life-threatening. That is, deficient performance, complaints from others and threats to authority may result in extreme harm to the child or to others if allowed to continue.

There's a second way to judge the severity of misbehavior from any cause. When we observe children doing things, our brains subconsciously (and often consciously) calculate the likely outcomes of their behaviors. We anticipate either good or bad consequences, their severity and most importantly, the approximate length of time till the consequence is likely to occur. When we anticipate *really bad* outcomes or *immediate* ill consequences, our emotions are more intense than when we anticipate either few or no ill consequences or judge the outcome of the behavior to be in the distant future.

Taking note of our emotional reaction to misbehavior provides a subjective, but valuable measure of its seriousness.

Three levels of emotion evoked by misbehavior fueled by anger

As we observe children misbehaving, we are likely to experience one or another of the following emotional reactions. I've grouped them into three levels because, in my experience, most observers are consistent in describing these reactions to a wide variety of children's misbehavior.

- annoyance

- Confusion, Anxiety, Anger

- FEAR

If we observe a child misbehaving in a fashion unlikely to cause harm, as for example breaking a pencil while doing homework or saying, "I hate you Mommy," when directed to turn off the TV, we're likely to feel annoyance, but unlikely to feel confusion, anxiety, anger or fear. In these situations, we calculate very little risk of a harmful outcome. Misbehaviors creating mere annoyance in the observer can be considered trivial in nature.

When we observe children cursing at us, bringing home failing grades from school or complaining of stomachaches when it's time to board the school bus, we're unlikely to experience mere annoyance. Rather we're likely to feel confusion, anxiety or anger, though not fear (at least at first). Misbehaviors reaching this level can be considered of moderate concern.

By contrast, the misbehaviors of overdosing on pills, threatening a classmate with a knife or torturing an animal are likely to exceed the first two categories and evoke fear. Misbehaviors reaching this level can be considered severe and potentially life-endangering.

Using combined objective and subjective measures of effects of misbehavior

Let's see how we can use the combination of affected Areas of Consequence (objective measures) and our level of emotional reaction to misbehavior (subjective measures) to judge its severity and guide us to managing it.

Here's that list of observed (objective) effects of misbehavior on Areas of Consequence:

- Inability to perform
  o Physical/body-related health (e.g.: stamina & strength)
  o Observed measures of intelligence (e.g.: milestones, grades)
  o Effects on social relationships

- Complaints from others

- Rule-breaking

And here's the list of emotions misbehavior typically evokes in observers:

- annoyance

- Confusion, Anxiety, Anger

- FEAR

As you might imagine, misbehavior blocking a child's ability to perform physically, intellectually or socially, may be due to potentially deadly conditions, like epilepsy, cancer, poisoning (including drug exposure or use) and many others.

Whenever any behavior is observed to block a child's performance within the Areas Consequence, serious disease may be present. In all such instances, a child specialist is best consulted to diagnose and treat the underlying cause(s). Such specialists include physicians, psychologists and educators.

Seize opportunities to ignore trivial misbehavior, no matter its cause

Here's an example of merely annoying behavior which, though appropriately described as misbehavior, fails to reach a level requiring an immediate response by parents. In general, if complaints are limited to only one other person and that person experiences only annoyance, misbehavior can be considered trivial and unworthy of any response – it can be safely ignored:

<u>Carey is 7 years old.</u> She insists on squirting catsup on all her food at every meal. She began doing this several days ago. When her parents ask her why she's doing this, she replies, "I like red food."

Carey is in second grade and doing well. She and her friends play cooperatively as always. At her last visit to the pediatrician, she was proclaimed a healthy child. No complaints have been received from school or from neighbors. Her parents find Carey's behavior at meal annoying, but they wisely decide to ignore it.

<u>Discussion:</u> None of the Areas of Consequence have been affected by Carey's behavior. No rule has been established in her household barring the use of catsup at meals. Only her parents seem to be annoyed with this behavior, but they realize they have the authority to ignore the behavior, thus consigning it to the trivial category.

Most serious & potentially dangerous forms of misbehavior affect ability to perform

Here's an example of violent misbehavior causing loss of skills and self-mutilation (a form of violent misbehavior) in a 2-1/2-year-old girl. The observed behaviors and the parents' emotional reactions to them progress from a moderate to a severe level of misbehavior:

Tilly enjoyed a healthy 9 month pregnancy and exhibited precocious developmental milestones till her second birthday. At that time her parents began to notice drooling, trouble getting a spoon into her mouth when eating and a degree of irritability previously uncharacteristic of their daughter. Her parents experienced confusion and anxiety as they observed Tilly's new behaviors. As a result, they consulted Tilly's pediatrician who advised further observation.

As time when on, Tilly became more irritable and engaged in frequent rages. She began twirling her hands and pulling out her hair. She stopped speaking to her parents. These behaviors evoked fear in the parents who then consulted a pediatric neurologist. The neurologist performed tests, including genetic analysis. Tilly was diagnosed with Rett Syndrome, a genetic disorder characterized by loss of previously acquired skills, seizures, self-mutilation and shortened life span.

Discussion: Tilly's behavior was characterized by a decline in all the skill areas of   performance,   thus qualifying as misbehavior. At first, her parents experienced anxiety and confusion. This combination of deficient performance and her parents moderate emotional reaction defined a moderate level of misbehavior worthy of assessment by a child specialist.

As further declines in performance, concerns voiced by others and threats to authority were observed, Tilly's parents became fearful, defining a severe level of misbehavior warranting immediate intervention. Unfortunately, Rett Syndrome is not curable and only supportive treatment is available to manage symptoms.

An easy way to choose child specialists for significant misbehavior

Over the years I've hit upon a simple way to decide which child specialist(s) to consult and in which order to see them. The process is much the same for professionals making this decision as it is for parents.

Medical doctors acting as primary care physicians, typically pediatricians, are best consulted first when deficiencies are observed in a child's physical performance. If subspecialists are required, for example neurologists, geneticists, gastroenterologists, your pediatrician is most likely to consult them in the most productive order.

Psychologists are best at assessing apparent deficits in intelligence and along with psychiatrists, are able to measure social-adaptive skills (relationships to others) and provide counseling, therapy and treatment strategies for underlying mental health disorders. Neither psychologists nor psychiatrists should be consulted before physical disorders have been ruled out.

Educators – teachers, reading, math, speech and language, occupational therapists – measure a child's achievement level, but not a child's intellectual ability. They provide supportive educational services once specific diagnoses have been made and they are best at tracking progress and response or lack of response to the intervention of medical doctors, psychiatrists and psychologists.

What have we learned so far?

Now we understand any form of misbehavior is identified by its objective effects on any of 3 Areas of Consequence – performance, effects on others and threats to authority. We see misbehavior is further defined by the subjective emotions evoked in the observer, ranging from trivial annoyance, through the moderate emotions of anger, confusion or anxiety to outright fear. Here's how to use the objective and subjective measures of misbehavior we just learned:

• Ignore trivial misbehavior recognized by its minimal effects on Areas of Consequence and the mere annoyance it evokes.

• STOP severe misbehavior immediately and forcefully, but legally, before spending time or effort on determining causes.

• Having limited any remaining misbehavior to the moderate level, we must next distinguish willful (defiant) from irreversible (brain-imposed) disorders as causes of misbehavior.

How to distinguish defiant (willful) misbehavior from brain-related misbehavior

To recognize defiant (willful) misbehavior, we look for anger as a byproduct of the defiance. Such behavior causes anger because it is designed (by the child) to manipulate us to do or accept something we don't want to do or accept – like allowing a child to stay up all night or miss a school bus – and targets only certain people or activities.

To recognize irreversible (brain-imposed) misbehavior, caused by underlying disorders not under a child's control, we look for the confusion or anxiety it evokes as we observe it. Such emotions are created by watching behaviors that are unpredictable, often directly harmful and which seem not to benefit the child in any way – like falling to the floor, shaking all over and wetting clothes or drooling.

Having distinguished defiant misbehavior from brain-imposed misbehavior, we enforce discipline on willful defiance and seek professional assistance for mental or physical disorders causing brain-imposed misbehavior not under the child's control.

In the next chapter, we'll complete our examination of violent behavior in children by looking at examples of these misbehaviors and seeing how the principles we've learned are applied to manage them.

Chapter Three

Applying the principles we've learned

Examples of violent misbehavior fueled by "curable" environmental situations

Angelina was first placed in foster care at 5 years of age when her parents, both drug-addicted, were found neglectful, having frequently left her unattended and alone at home. She was then placed with 3 successive foster families, one of which had been investigated and suspected of physically and possibly sexually abusing her at 6 years of age.

Angelina was 9 years of age when her foster parents brought her to my office. They were fearful of a pattern of violent behaviors both at school and at home. These included breaking pencils and crayons, throwing items at teachers and classmates, hitting and fighting on the school bus and, most recently, stabbing her Foster Mom with a pencil during a rage. The parents had just received notice of Angelina's transfer to a school for emotionally disturbed children.

Her parents indicated Angelina seemed bright and could be affectionate, but she responded to any imposed restrictions with anger, which quickly progressed to rage and aggression.

Managing Angelina's complex misbehavior including violence:

• Judge the severity of the misbehavior.

We can ignore trivial levels of misbehavior and must STOP intense levels without delay. Only when misbehavior is limited to moderate levels will we have time to distinguish defiant from brain-related forms and develop strategies to manage it.

• Check effects on the objective Areas of Consequence:

Angelina's behavior threatens Performance within the area of social relationships, generates complaints from Others and threatens Authority.

Check the level of emotionality evoked by the misbehavior:

The parents are experiencing fear as they observe Angelina's misbehavior.

Threats to all 3 of the Areas of Consequence, along with the parents' subjective reaction of FEAR, Angelina's misbehavior falls at an intense level and must be stopped immediately. Intense, life-endangering misbehavior leaves no time to determine causes or to develop disciplinary strategies. The school's decision to enroll Angelina in a program for emotionally disturbed children cannot be expected to provide immediate safety for all concerned.

Managing Angelina's complex misbehavior including violence

Here's what we did: Angelina's parents called 911 after Mom was stabbed with a pencil. Angelina was transported to a local child psychiatric crisis unit for close observation and initial treatment. During her 3 day stay, she acknowledged "losing my temper too easily. I keep thinking about bad things and people make me scared and angry."

In the crisis unit Angelina began working with a therapist. She began describing specific abusive events from her past. After 3 days, she was discharged with a diagnosis of Post-Traumatic Stress Disorder (PTSD).

• Douse the violence: Think sparks, tinder, fuel

Fuel: Post Traumatic Stress Disorder due to past abuse

Tinder: Anger too easily aroused

Sparks: Normal demands of daily living

Neither Angelina's therapist nor her foster parents were able to remove the sparks igniting Angelina's anger. Rather, they targeted the tinder and fuel responsible for creating violent behavior. A mood stabilizing medication was prescribed to slow the progression of anger to rage while her therapist taught her anger-management strategies.

As she became more adept at managing anger flare-ups, Angelina's medication doses were lowered and eventually stopped. She returned to a mainstream school where she resumed achieving above average grades and relating well to her parents and classmates.

<u>Byron, age 12 years, was referred to my office by the Court</u> and appeared with his Mom and Case Worker while residing in Juvenile Detention.

Mom related Byron had been transferred from his mainstream school to a school for emotionally disturbed children. Soon after his Dad had abandoned the family 2 years earlier, Byron had been suspended from school several times for assaultive bullying of classmates and stealing from his teachers. These behaviors, occurring both at home and at school, continued to worsen and culminated in his setting fire to a school bathroom. A

911 call from the school led to his incarceration in a Juvenile Detention Center and his referral to my office.

Byron's Mom, a single parent, expressed fear that she or Byron's younger brother, cerebral palsied and wheelchair-bound, might be harmed during Byron's rages. She related Byron had threatened to burn down their home. Byron's unpredictable rages, Mom also related, created feelings of constant anxiety and confusion.

Managing Byron's complex misbehavior including violence

Here's what we did:

• We judged the severity of Byron's misbehavior

• We began by checking threats to the Areas of Consequence:

Byron's behavior threatened Performance within the area of social relationships generated complaints from Others and threatened Authority.

We checked the level of emotionality evoked by the misbehavior:

Byron's Mom expressed anxiety, confusion and FEAR.

Threats to all 3 of the Areas of Consequence, along with Mom's subjective reactions of confusion anxiety and FEAR, placed Byron's misbehavior at an intense level and required immediate cessation. Intense, life-endangering misbehavior leaves no time to determine causes or to develop disciplinary strategies.

As we've also seen, reactions of confusion and anxiety suggest underlying brain-related causes for misbehavior requiring the help of child specialists. But, the severe level of Byron's misbehavior left no time to distinguish between defiant vs. brain related disorders. His threat to burn his home down had to be taken seriously and releasing him to his residence from Juvenile Detention was too risky to contemplate.

• We took steps to douse the violence: Think sparks, tinder, fuel

Fuel: Possible underlying mental health disorder

Tinder: Younger disabled brother consuming most of Mom's attention. Dad's abandonment of the family 2 years earlier.

Sparks: Demands of school, daily activities.

With Mom's agreement, we arranged to admit Byron to a longer-term, state financed residential psychiatric treatment facility.

After a 4 month stay, Byron emerged with a confirmed diagnosis of Adjustment Disorder and an associated Mood Disorder. Family therapy sessions   immediately after his release from the residential facility focused on Byron's complaints of "being ignored by his Mom," and his anger related to Dad's abandonment.

Ongoing prescriptions for fluoxetine, an antidepressant, and valproic acid, an anticonvulsant mood stabilizer, allowed Byron to manage his anger while his therapist gradually equipped Byron to express affection for his family.

Examples of violence as a byproduct of underlying physical or mental health conditions ("treatable", though not "curable")

Rachel was 15 years old when she was brought to my office by her Mom. She was born prematurely and experienced seizures in the nursery. Her Dad abandoned the family before Rachel's first birthday.

Rachel began walking at 2 years of age and began using 2 word phrases at 4 years of age. These observations placed Rachel's performance at about 1/2 of her age. She was enrolled in a preschool and periodic measures of performance were shared with her Mom.

By 6 years of age, Rachel performed like a 3-year-old and by 10 years of age, like a 5-year-old. She had just begun menstrual periods. Her measured, overall IQ was measured at 50 (mental retardation is generally defined as below 70 IQ points.)

Mom described Rachel to me as "a usually loving child" who gave and received affection with her Mom and usually with her teachers. But, for the past year, Rachel had begun reacting to any limitations on play or meals or any unwanted assistance with dressing or personal hygiene by hitting or biting Mom, teachers or caretakers. She would often scream, "I'm a big girl!" Her Mom related, "She can change from happy to raging in a flash!"

Mom admitted Rachel's behavior often angered her. At other times, Mom felt confused that Rachel would target her with violence. Because Rachel was a large girl, her Mom expressed fear she might seriously injure someone, be expelled from school or even arrested.

Managing Rachel's complex misbehavior including violence

Here's what we did:

- We judged the severity of Rachel's misbehavior

- We began by checking threats to the Areas of Consequence:

Rachel's behaviors exhibited deficient performance (already well defined on IQ testing as mental retardation), targeted others (Mom, teachers and caretakers) and threatened authority (rules like not biting or hitting).

- We noted the emotions evoked by these behaviors

Mom expressed confusion over Rachel's targeting her with violence, but also fear of Rachel's arrest.

Threats to all of the Areas of Consequence and the evoking of fear raised the level of Rachel's misbehavior to an intense level requiring immediate control. As in previous examples, confusion as a reaction to misbehavior suggests underlying brain-related disturbances, while anger suggests a defiant (willful) component to the behavior.

- We took steps to douse the violence: Think sparks, tinder, fuel

Fuel: Mental retardation with underlying brain abnormalities. Adolescent body changes in a child with mental age of 7-1/2.

Tinder: Unrealistic expectations by family and caretakers for child's mental age.

Sparks: Demands of activities of daily living.

Rachel exhibited indications of both an underlying brain-related disorder, confusion on Mom's part, as well as indications of willful misbehavior (anger on Mom's part) reaffirming the contributions of mental retardation and also inappropriate, willful decision making on her part. Rachel's choice to bite when stressed required immediate management.

Rachel was fitted with a football helmet, including face guard, to block biting of others. Snaps on the helmet were crimped to make it difficult for her to remove the helmet without assistance. She was advised she'd have to wear the helmet till she learned to control her anger. To achieve this goal, Rachel was enrolled in a Cognitive Behavioral Therapy program through a local mental health agency. She was highly motivated to learn anger management strategies (tailored to her mental age) because she hated wearing the helmet.

Within 6 weeks, Rachel stopped biting and learned to say, "You're making me angry" when appropriate. Rachel's therapist focused her efforts on enhancing Rachel's Activities of Daily Living, including personal hygiene.

<u>Jose' was 5 years old, exhibiting intensifying periods of spontaneous and aggressive rages</u> when he visited my office. He had just been discharged from a local child psychiatric crisis unit.

Jose' had enjoyed a normal infancy and childhood till his entry into kindergarten. But during the past several months, his parents saw gradually intensifying anger flare-ups, most of which seemed to occur without any trigger. He also experienced periods of extreme hyperactivity. Jose' could be enjoying a fun activity, then might suddenly become enraged. Rages lasted 5 – 10 minutes, then Jose' would typically fall asleep. When he woke up, he'd act as if nothing had happened, almost as if he had no memory of the episode.

Jose's teacher also began reporting frequent anger flare-ups, often associated with throwing objects and breaking things. She said, "I have to walk on eggshells because almost any request I make might trigger a violent reaction." A crisis point was reached when Jose stabbed another child with a pencil during a sudden rage, resulting a 911 call from the school. His parents were advised by a police officer to accompany them to a nearby psychiatric crisis unit.

Managing Jose's complex misbehavior including violence

The management of Jose's violent misbehavior was initiated before I first saw him. But the sequence of events followed the same steps we've already examined:

- The severity of Jose's misbehavior was determined

  o Threats to Areas of Consequence included the social skill area performance as well as threats to others and authority.

  o Emotions evoked by Jose's misbehavior included fear.

These observations defined a severe level of misbehavior requiring immediate control.

With the stabbing of a classmate, Jose's teacher very appropriately recognized a potentially life-threatening level of violent misbehavior and called 911. Jose' was transported to a local child psychiatric crisis unit.

At the crisis unit, Jose' exhibited manic periods (sustained "hyperactivity") and spontaneous episodes of unprovoked anger. Many of his anger flare-ups progressed to violent rages, during which the staff psychiatrist observed epileptic-like behavior. A brainwave test (EEG) was normal, eliminating epilepsy as the diagnosis. Jose' was diagnosed with Bipolar Disorder with Psychogenic, Non-Epileptic Seizures (PNES) – a brain abnormality resembling epilepsy and often responsive to medications used for epilepsy.

• Jose's violent misbehavior was doused: Think spark, tinder, fuel

Fuel: Brain abnormalities – Bipolar Disorder and PNES

Tinder: Manic periods and spontaneous anger

Sparks: Normal demands of daily life

Jose's Bipolar Disorder and PNES are both non-curable conditions which can fuel violent misbehavior. Though non-curable, they are treatable with medications that stabilize mood and reduce the intensity of anger.

Jose' violent behavior was successfully treated with oxcarbazepine, an anticonvulsant mood stabilizer, and risperidone, an antipsychotic medication.

By the time his Mom brought him to my office, Jose' had resumed satisfactory school activities and required only management of his medications.

Chapter Four

An approach to managing violent behavior

In the preceding chapters, we've learned to recognize misbehavior by examining Areas of Consequence, to judge its intensity by combining affected Areas of Consequence with the type and intensity of emotion evoked by the misbehavior and ignoring trivial misbehavior while stopping intense levels of violence immediately and with whatever degree of legal force is required.

We've also learned misbehavior can be broadly divided into 2 categories, each of which is managed differently. We've seen one form of misbehavior is willful (defiant), representing conscious though inappropriate decision-making on a child's part. Another form of misbehavior is caused by brain-imposed disorders over which a child has little or no control.

We've learned willful (defiant) misbehavior tends to evoke feelings of anger while brain-imposed disorders tend to evoke feelings of anxiety or confusion. And we've seen a child may suffer from both varieties of misbehavior at the same time, evoking both anger and anxiety or confusion (e.g.: a diabetic child who purposefully overdoses on insulin on schooldays to avoid having to attend school).

The astute reader may have noted we haven't talked much about managing moderate, willful levels of misbehavior, violent or otherwise. Moderate misbehavior of a willful (defiant) nature is managed with discipline. The author discusses disciplining moderate, willful misbehavior in a separate publication, <u>Discipline Your Child...without going to jail</u>.

Now, let's summarize the steps we've learned to recognize, categorize and manage violent misbehavior in children:

Check objective Areas of Consequence for threats posed by the behavior-

- Inability to perform age-level activities
  o Physical/body-related health (e.g.: stamina & strength)
  o Observed measures of intelligence (e.g.: milestones, grades)
  o Effects on social relationships
- Complaints from others

• Threats to authority (rule-breaking)

Note subjective evoked emotional responses

• annoyance – trivial level

• Anxiety, Confusion, Anger – moderate level

• FEAR – intense level

Combine objective and subjective measure of misbehavior:

• Ignore trivial misbehavior.

• (Discipline moderate levels of misbehavior, violent or otherwise).

• STOP intense, violent misbehavior with whatever legal force is needed.

In the examples presented in Chapter Three, 911 calls were often required to stop dangerous, violent misbehavior. This approach is often required for older, physically menacing children. Though incarceration may initially follow, diagnosis and treatment usually requires assessment by child specialists in a secure environment. Admission to a local children's psychiatric crisis unit or even placement in a residential center may be required. Returning a violently misbehaving youngster to an insecure environment is neither a compassionate nor a loving approach.

Suggested Reading/Resources

1. Discipline Your Child...without going to jail, A. Davick, M.D., 2015

2. ADHD: What every parent should know, A. Davick, M.D. 2016

3. Managing Misbehavior in Kids: The MIS/Kidding® Process, A. Davick, M.D., 2014

4. Bullying Rarely Travels Alone, A. Davick, M.D. 2014

5. Dr. Davick's blog – Questions, comments, answers:

www.Managing MisbehaviorInKids.com

6. Dr. Davick's digital and printed publications:

www.DrDavick.com

Dr. Alan Davick

About the Author

Dr. Alan Davick, a Developmental-Behavioral Pediatrician, has taught parents and professional colleagues how to recognize and manage complex misbehavior in children for 40 years. Trained at the Johns Hopkins Medical Institutions, Dr. Davick has maintained clinical practice throughout those years. He has, as a Major in the Army Medical Corps, served as Pediatrician-in-Chief at Tuttle Army Health Clinic, Savannah GA and later, while engaged in private Pediatric practice, as Behavioral-Developmental Consultant to the Chatsworth School for Exceptional Children, in Baltimore County, MD.

Dr. Davick has focused his knowledge and experience on separating innate conditions like ADHD, Bipolar Disorder, Cerebral Palsy, Developmental Delay and Epilepsy, masquerading as willful misbehavior, from truly volitional misconduct, like Oppositional-Defiant Disorder and Conduct Disorders.

In Violence in Children, Dr. Davick shows the reader how to recognize, categorize and manage violent misbehavior.

Dr. Davick lives with his wife, Barbara, in Cape Coral, FL, where he practices Child Psychiatry.

www.DrDavick.com

Ordering Information

Managing Misbehavior in Kids: The MIS/Kidding Process – A Professionals' Manual
© 2013 Alan M. Davick, M.D.
ISBN: 978-09890053-0-2

Bullying Rarely: Travels Alone
© 2014 Alan M. Davick, M.D.
ISBN: 978-09890053-2-6

Discipline Your Child: Without Going to Jail
© 2015 Alan M. Davick, M.D.
ISBN: 978-0-9890053-6-4

ADHD: What Every Parent Should Know
© 2015 Alan M. Davick, M.D.
ISBN: 978-0-9890053-8-8

For more information about Dr. Davick's books, please send your queries to:

Alan M. Davick, M.D.
MISKIDDING, LLC
P.O. Box 101127
Cape Coral, FL 33910-1127
URL: www.DrDavick.com
Blog: www. MisbehviorInKids.com